D1585391

LANCASTER

A BOMBING LEGEND

LANCASTER
A BOMBING LEGEND

Rick Radell & Mike Vines

OSPREY
AEROSPACE

Published in 1993 by Osprey Publishing
81 Fulham Road, London SW3 6RB

© Osprey Publishing

ISBN 1 85532 267 6

Edited by Tony Holmes
Page design by Paul Kime
Cutaway Swanborough Associates copyright
Line drawings Dennis Punnett copyright

Printed in China

Front cover The BBMF Lancaster B
Mk 1 tucks in behind the RAF
Andover photo-ship as the pair skirt
around the Channel Islands

Back cover The groundcrew
rearrange the contents of the BBMF
hangar at RAF Coningsby prior to
carefully pushing PA474 back
inside. An ominous thunderstorm
provides the dramatic backdrop for
this atmospheric photograph

Title page With a maximum
allowable boost rate of 18 lbs, VR-
A's crew maintain specific operating
parameters. On take-off a setting of
2950 rpm, +9 lbs boost, is used,
whilst at cruising altitude 2200 rpm,
+2 lbs boost, is applied. A maximum
continuous power setting of 2650
rpm, +7 lbs boost, can be achieved.
Flying VR-A to its engineered limits
is not a requirement of today's
operations

Right The BBMF are the most
popular visitors to the Channel
Islands Battle of Britain air display
every year, which for the benefit of
holiday makers is held on a Friday.
The older Islanders who suffered
four years of Nazi occupation from
28 June 1940, and who still
remember the great sacrifices that
were made in those hard times, jam
the roads around the airport to see
the Lancaster, Spitfire and
Hurricane. When the air-to-air sortie
was being planned I suggested
flying over some of the Channel
Islands' jagged coastline to give
extra drama to the shots. Jersey Air
Traffic immediately came back with,
'Well you can operate over Sark for
as long as you want. I can guarantee
that the locals won't complain!' The
aircraft had been flown into Jersey
Airport earlier in the morning
after being forced back to
Bournemouth (Hurn) by bad
weather the day before

Acknowledgements

Mike Vines wishes to thank the following individuals for their help during the compilation of this volume; Sqn Ldr Andy Tomalin, CO of the BBMF, for putting up with him on his many visits to Coningsby, and for his patience in answering every question that the author threw at him; to his entire team of enthusiastic and hard working groundcrew for keeping these magnificent aircraft flying for us all to see; and to Michael Hill and his team at Strike Command PR, who fixed the air-to-air sorties, especially the Channel Islands shoot, which was cleared within two days of asking for the facility. Grateful thanks also to Simon Morris of Dunn's Photographic Laboratories for his fast and consistent service; to Ted Frankland of Fuji Photo Film (UK) Ltd, Professional Photographic Division, for his advice and help; and to Paul Thomas of Keith Johnson and Pelling Ltd for the loan of the specialist lenses.

All photographs in the BBMF chapters were shot on Fuji 100D or Fuji Velvia film loaded in Pentax 6 x 7 and Nikon F3 and F4 cameras.

Every effort has been made to list those individuals or organizations that were so kind in assisting Rick Radell with his research on the Mynarski Memorial Lancaster. Thanks to the Canadian Warplane Heritage Museum; the Lancaster Support Club; No 419 'Moose' Sqn; George and Irene Sobering; the Association of Living History, Dayton, Ohio; John and Daphne Balfour; John Cummins; Bob Fraser; Larry Melling; Harry Huffman; Norman 'Kit' Carson; Gil Hunt; Doug Brown; Steve Martin; Ron Wylie; Margaret Mathers; Margaret Sutherland; Carl Haycock; Greg Hanna; Don Schofield; Sally Maderich; Ron Kaye; Gord Hill; Karl Coolen; Doug Bentley; Wilf Riddle; Norman Shrive; Stew Brickenden; Bill McBride; Howard Pardue; Kermit Weeks; and Fred Passmore. Special thanks to Dennis Bradley; Jack Evans; Richard Palimaka; Al Topham; Darlene McKinnon; Al Mickeloff; Cy Dunbar; Rick Franks; Bill Randall; Bob Hill; the 'Beech Boys'; Paul Cronkwright; Bob McKinnon; Rob Schweyer; and last, but by no means least, my wife Martha for her support and patience.

About the authors

Rick Radell is a professional photographer with a degree in photographic technology from Ryerson Polytechnical Institute, Toronto, Canada. His involvement in the field of aviation as a private pilot, coupled with his passion for vintage aircraft, brought about the marriage of two perfectly natural talents. Rick's outstanding images have been the nucleus for the most sought after aviation calendar in Canada, *Canadian Vintage Aircraft*. He is also a contributing writer and photo-editor for the Canadian Warplane Heritage Museum's *Flightlines* magazine.

Mike Vines started photographing aeroplanes with his 'box brownie' from about the age of 14. After his first few pictures were published in aviation magazines he was totally hooked. After leaving school he worked for a year in a photographic studio, before joining the Ministry of Defence as a photographer/air observer. After seven years with the MoD, he ran a large multi-national photographic unit, working as a freelance aviation 'sharpshooter' in his spare time. In 1990 Mike took the plunge and set up his own company, *Photo Link*, which specialises in aviation images. He is an official photographer for the Shuttleworth Collection, and a member of the British Institute of Professional Photographers. His work appears regularly in *Pilot* and *Aeroplane Monthly*, as well as in periodicals in Europe and the USA. *Lancaster – A Bombing Legend* is Mike's fourth book for Osprey.

Right VR-A shows off its massive wingspan as the bomber turns over Lake Erie just minutes from its home base at Mount Hope. With a wing span of 102 ft, and an encompassing wing area of 1297 sq ft, the Lancaster had the capability of carrying the greatest weapons load of any allied bomber during World War 2

Contents

Pre-season

You must have felt the atmosphere! A sharp-eyed youngster in the crowd spots the classic silhouette as it orbits 'off-stage' waiting for its cue. The initial babble of excitement is replaced by an almost religious hush at the arrival of the only airworthy Avro Lancaster on this side of the Atlantic.

The proud veterans watching from the ground, some of whom will have flown half way around the world for this moment, wait for the unmistakable throb of four Merlins. Ex-groundcrew members, doubtless re-living the hours they waited for 'their' bombers to return after a mission, go misty eyed as the memories flood back.

For the 'youngsters' the term bomber means Lancaster, and they would all agree that this was simply the greatest bomber ever built. And who could argue with them; the Lancaster had the most trouble free introduction into service of probably any type of aircraft during World War 2. Even its designer, AV Roe's Roy Chadwick, was astounded at the way it met every target it was set.

The last airworthy Lancaster in the UK, PA474 is operated by the Battle of Britain Memorial Flight (BBMF), who share RAF Coningsby, in Lincolnshire, with several Tornado F.3 squadrons. The BBMF also operates five Spitfires and a Hurricane, and the sight of these classic fighters escorting the Lancaster is guaranteed to turn the head of even the most seasoned airshow goer.

As CO of the Flight, Sqn Ldr Andy Tomalin, RAF, is the only full-time pilot with the unit. The aircrew under his command are all serving officers at Coningsby, instructing on the Tornado F.3. The Lancaster's air engineers are drawn from a pool of three officers from nearby RAF Finningley. Eighteen full-time RAF groundcrew make up the rest of the team, under the watchful eye of the engineering officer, Warrant Officer Barry Sears.

PA474 was built by Vickers Armstrongs at Chester in 1945 to B Mk 1 (FE) (Far East) specification, and was intended for use with Tiger Force, the joint Anglo/US operation against the Japanese following the cessation of hostilities in Europe.

Right The Lancaster's lair. The dark shape of the bomber is always impressive, but up close it can be seen that PA474 is minus its port outer propeller, which is away being worked on. During ground tests the day before the prop would not come out of 'feather', a problem which had not occurred in the aircraft's previous flight. The fault was cured a few days later though by switching parts from the BBMF's stores 'vault'

Above CO of the BBMF and pilot of the Lancaster, Sqn Ldr Andy Tomalin (at the overhead projector) briefs the Spitfire and Hurricane pilots, as well as the groundcrew members, for a flight to Royal Naval Air Station Yeovilton, with a display at RAF Upper Heyford, Oxfordshire, en route. The safe operation of the Flight dictates that the sortie can only take place in VFR (Visual Flight Rules) conditions, with a maximum wind speed of 25 kts and a maximum 15 kt cross-wind for take-offs and landings. The Lancaster usually cruises at around 150/170 kts, burning around 200 gallons of fuel per hour. The minimum display height is 100 ft, and no manoeuvres in excess of +1.8 G are permitted

Right The flight engineer for this trip is Flt Lt Mike Vickers, whose main panel is on the starboard side of the rear cockpit. He is responsible for the fuel management of the aircraft, and his time is spent monitoring fuel contents, engine oil and cooling temperatures, and because of the close proximity of the nav's table (left), he is usually to be seen crouching or standing by the bank of dials whilst the bomber is airborne. Wartime flight engineers were trained by their pilots to be able to fly the aircraft straight and level in case of an emergency

Events in the Far East out-paced the need for the aircraft, and in 1947 it was converted to perform the photo recon role, joining No 82 Sqn in 1948 for the photographic survey of West Africa.

Returning to the UK in 1952, PA474 was scheduled for pilotless drone conversion, but on the 17 March 1954 the bomber was flown to the College of Aeronautics at Cranfield instead. Now tasked with the role of flying test bed, the aircraft was used in laminar flow research, with test wing sections mounted atop its fuselage.

On retirement from Cranfield, PA474 was first stored at No 15 Maintenance Unit at Wroughton, where it was restored in wartime colours (without any squadron or identification markings). The bomber went on to feature in the motion pictures *The Guns of Navarone* and *Operation Crossbow* during this sojourn in Wiltshire.

In the early 1960s it looked like PA474 would be going to the RAF Museum at Hendon as a static exhibit, but a flight to RAF Waddington in 1965 saved it from this fate. The plan was to form a static memorial, but Waddington-based No 44 (Rhodesia) Sqn (the first unit to operate the Lancaster) had other ideas, and with volunteer help, restored the aircraft to its former flying glory. In 1973 PA474 joined what was then the Battle of Britain Flight at RAF Coltishall.

Visitors can view the Lancaster's lair at Coningsby five days a week (except on bank holidays and during the two-week Christmas season) from 10.00 am until 5.00 pm (last entry into the hangar at 3.30 pm). Entry to the exhibition and souvenir shop is free, but there is a small charge for guided tours of the hangar. There is no guarantee that a particular aircraft will be there on a specific day though, so you are invited to phone Coningsby (0526 344041) before setting out.

Right After a pre-season engine run PA474 is pushed back into the warmth of the hangar before a rain storm roars through Coningsby. Handled gently, and with only about 78 hours flying time being logged each year, the aircraft has still got a life expectancy of 3500 hours, allowing PA474 to continue flying through to the year 2036! The Lancaster is highly revered both in Britain and across the Commonwealth due to the exploits of Allied crews over Europe in World War 2. At its peak, the aircraft equipped no less than 56 RAF squadrons within Bomber Command, these units being directly responsible for taking the fight back to the enemy in so many spectacular night raids. By the end of 1942 the Lancaster had proven itself capable of reaching the furthest targets at speeds of 240 kts and altitudes of between 22,000 and 27,000 ft, carrying a bomb load of around 8000 lbs

Above PA474 shows off its inboard and outboard split trailing edge flaps, whilst Spitfire Mk IIA P7350 gets inspected by visitors on a hangar tour. P7350 was damaged in a landing accident during the 1992 airshow season at RAF Chivenor when the Merlin lost power soon after take-off. The aircraft sustained undercarriage, airframe and propeller damage, but pilot Sqn Ldr Paul Day escaped unhurt

Left Engine technician Cpl Nigel Bunn (known as 'sticky' to his friends) checks out the mighty Merlin with junior technician Fiona Holding, while SAC Danny Smith checks out the No 2 powerplant prior to the aircraft being rolled out for engine runs. The Lancaster became the most successful RAF bomber of the war, having a superior performance in range, height, speed and bomb carrying ability over all of its competitors. From its sickly childhood as the twin-engined Avro Manchester, the Lancaster was transformed into a war winner through the replacement of the former's unreliable Rolls-Royce Vulture engines with four Rolls Royce Merlins, which were fitted to a new lengthened wing

It is as if the aircraft in the BBMF hangar can sense the start of a new season. P7350 watches while PA474 gets some final attention before the springtime engine runs. Theoretically, the period between October and Christmas is the quietest time for the BBMF, the engineers usually conducting major airframe and engine inspections during the autumn months. After the New Year however, the aircraft have to be readied for flying; the 1993 season started in February (a good month earlier than usual) so as to fully prepare the BBMF for the first major flypast to celebrate the 75th anniversary of the RAF on 1 April 1993. Unexpected snags can turn into major problems, and sometimes after a ground run or an air test, it is all hands on deck and plenty of late nights for everyone in an effort to get the flight serviceable again

Above It's not just the general public who enjoy visiting the BBMF hangar – often you see RAF personnel, as well as visiting foreign aircrews, making a bee-line for the oldies. On the right a visiting group of journalists are shown the Lancaster at close quarters by the Flight's CO

Left PA474 proudly wears its City of Lincoln crest as it is run up on the BBMF pan, the engine cowls having been taken off to ease the inspection process and allow the groundcrew to thoroughly check for oil leaks. Some of Coningsby's Tornado F.3s can be seen being readied for flight in the background. When visiting the base you never quite get over the shock of seeing the Flight's veteran machines sharing ramp space with the RAF's most potent interceptors

Above A relieved Sqn Ldr Andy Tomalin waits for the hangar doors to be fully opened at the start of a new season's flying. PA474 logs about 78 hours a year displaying at over 150 events. Requests for a sight of the aircraft outweigh the time available, but single flypasts are fitted in wherever possible en route to other major events

Right Visitors are dwarfed (or is it swallowed) by the aircraft's cavernous 33 ft by 5 ft bomb bay. The Lancaster was arguably the most effective heavy bomber of the war as it could deliver 14,000 lbs of bombs over a range of 1660 miles, or one gigantic 22,000lb Grand Slam earthquake device over a range of 1040 miles. According to Sir Arthur 'Bomber' Harris, 'the Lancaster was the greatest single factor in winning the war. Its efficiency was almost incredible, both in performance and in the way it could be saddled with ever-increasing loads without breaking this camel's back. The Lancaster was the only aircraft in the world capable of lifting the 22,000 lb Grand Slam bomb; neither the Halifax or Stirling could carry anything like 12,000 lbs, let alone twice that amount. Not only could it take heavier bomb loads; not only was it easier to handle; and not only were there fewer accidents with it than with other types, the casualty rate was also consistently below those of other types'. But even so the cost in terms of aircrew was high – of the 7374 Lancasters built, more than 3000 failed to return from operational sorties, resulting in the deaths of 47,000 Bomber Command aircrew; this total accounts for a staggering 66 per cent of all RAF losses during World War 2

Above The BBMF crew disembark from the *City of Lincoln* after an approval flight for Air Vice Marshal John Allison, who is himself a warbirds pilot in his spare time. The approval display has to be flown each year before the start of the airshow season to clear the men, machines and manoeuvres before they are allowed to perform in public

Right If you are ever lucky enough to see the start-up procedure of a Lancaster, watch out for one of the groundcrew members vanishing up and into the wheel wells. Armed with a priming pump, he is squirting a neat mixture of fuel into each cylinder before the starter is applied; both wheel wells have priming pumps. The No 3, or starboard-inner engine, is always started first as it drives the compressor supplying air pressure for the brakes and radiator shutters

Above The Air Gunners Association badge is bolted to the rear Frazer-Nash gun turret of PA474 as a permanent memorial to all of those brave men who defended their aircraft, often against incredible odds. Once in the turrets, weighed down in electrically-heated flying suits, thick flying clothing, 'Mae Wests' and parachute harnesses, the gunner was left with very little room in which to 'stretch out' on the long flights to and from the target

Left The rear turret was the loneliest and coldest place in the aircraft as the gunner's only contact with the rest of the crew was via the intercom. Enemy attacks, when they came, were usually from the rear, as the nightfighters would try to kill the rear-gunner first before finishing off the virtually undefended aircraft. If the Lancaster had already dropped its bomb load, and the rear-gunner was fit and well, then the rest of the crew had at least half a chance of survival. The bomber was a remarkably agile machine for its size, and could be jinked and dived at alarming angles when avoiding an attack. However, despite its relative manoeuvrability, the Lancaster usually lost the services of the rear turret after about 20 seconds if the enemy aircraft carried home its attack

Above 'After flighting' is as necessary as pre-flighting on an aircraft this size. The groundcrew member is looking for oil and fuel leaks, or anything else that may have come adrift, as he walks the 102 ft of the Lancaster's wing. The massive flying surface doubles as the fuel tank for the aircraft, and it can carry up to 2154 Imperial gallons in its six tanks. The groundcrew are all volunteers, and none of them seem to complain despite the rumoured high work load and weekends away during the display season, which starts in April and goes through until September

Right Built as a power operated unit by Frazer-Nash, the rear turret on PA474 is now manually configured as the hydraulic actuating gear was removed some years ago to reduce weight and to cut down on maintenance requirements; the 0.303 Brownings can still be traversed however. The rear gunner had 10,000 rounds of ammunition with him for his quartet of 0.303 Brownings

Left A Canadian Packard 225 is presently residing under the No 2 cowling of PA474. This particular engine was built to power wartime Mosquitos, and was bought from the Strathallan Collection, overhauled and fitted in the Lancaster in 1988. Flame damping exhaust shrouds, which were vital in hiding the aircraft's position from enemy fighters during the night bomber offensive, are not fitted to this machine. PA474 is normally flown at +7 boost at 3000 rpm, although the engines could produce twice that amount in an emergency

Above PA474 taxies back to its dispersal after another successful display. The BBMF, or The Battle of Britain Flight as it was earlier known when set up in 1957, · originally comprised three Spitfires and one Hurricane. The Lancaster joined the Flight in 1973, and the word 'Memorial' was added to the titling to accommodate the machine. So apart from all of the official anniversaries to be held in 1993, it is also PA474's 20th year with the BBMF

Above The Lancaster is an impressive beast from most angles, but head on with the bomb doors open it looks exactly right for the job. On 27 January 1941 (only 18 days after its first flight) the prototype Lancaster was delivered to Aeroplane and Armament Experimental Establishment (A & AEE) at Boscombe Down for acceptance trials. It achieved the best assessment ever awarded to a new aircraft, and in the A & AEE's words, 'This aeroplane is eminently suitable for operational service'. PA474's engines from right to left, or one to four as they are known by the crews, consist of two Rolls-Royce Merlin 502s in the Nos 1 and 4 positions, a Merlin 25 at No 3 and a Packard 225 in the No 2 slot. The Lancaster's Merlins are interchangeable with the BBMF's Hurricane powerplant, as Sgt Dave Payne explained. 'The No 1 engine came from Hurricane LF363, having been removed from the fighter in 1971 and fitted in the Lancaster in 1974. When the engine 'life expired' at 1000 hours in 1987 it was removed, overhauled and zero houred, before being re-fitted to the Lanc in 1990'. The No 3 engine was acquired in 1988 from a private owner, whilst the No 4 Merlin was fitted to PA474 from 1975 until 1987, the powerplant then being removed, 'life-exed', overhauled and re-fitted four years later. The BBMF has a total of 13 Merlin/Packards on the books, seven of which can be switched easily from the Lancaster to the Hurricane. The Flight are always looking to increase their spares holding for all of their aircraft so if you know anyone who might wish to donate equipment please get them to contact the BBMF

Right Co-pilot Sqn Ldr Steve Bridger has opened his sliding side window to check that the tarmac around the bomber is clear of obstacles; the cockpit sits 20 ft above the ground when the Lancaster is resting on its sturdy undercarriage

Above Underneath the nose turret is the bomb-aimer's position, complete with gold fish bowl and angled optical flat, with the bomb sight fixed on top. Giving the emergency floor hatch a swift kick was always recommended before putting your full weight on it. The bomb aimer's other job was manning the forward gun turret before and after the 'run'. The grey rectangular box on the left side of the compartment is the electrical control box for the F.24 camera, which was used to assess the accuracy of the ordnance dropped

Left *City of Lincoln* is unusual in having dual controls, which enables pilot conversion to be achieved more easily. A red control lock is fixed to the control column in this picture, and the co-pilot's folding seat is just visible at bottom right

Above Sqn Ldr Andy Tomalin looks around to see if the crew are ready for start-up. Prior to joining the Flight, Andy flew Victor tankers with No 214 Sqn for six years, before moving on to become a flying instructor, where he flew just about every RAF type then in the inventory. Recalled to Victors during the Falklands campaign, he has now amassed over 6000 flying hours. Behind Andy is the navigator for this trip, Flt Lt Jerry Uren, who is currently serving in this capacity as an instructor with No 229 OCU, flying in the back seat of the unit's Tornado F.3s

Left Not the place for those who suffer from claustrophobia! The very cramped conditions in the rear Frazer-Nash turret, which is seen opened sideways, leave you marvelling at the sheer guts of the gunners. Not only did they have to be physically tough enough to fight in this position, they also had to have enough mental resilience to withstand the loneliness and cold that was the rear-gunner's lot. The bomber made its service debut with No 44 Sqn on 3 March 1942 when the unit performed minelaying sorties over the Heligoland Bight. A week later a pair of Lancasters from the same unit dropped 10,100 lbs of incendiaries on Essen, thus 'blooding' the aircraft in its more familiar bombing role

Above The BBMF crew room, as you would expect, is covered in memorabilia – even the walls of the corridors leading to it are covered in framed prints of the Flight's aircraft. Pictured left to right are Sqn Ldr Andy Tomalin (who doesn't like having his picture taken much), navigator Flt Lt Jerry Uren, Sqn Ldr Jim Wild (the pilot of the Flight's de Havilland Devon C.2) and Sqn Ldr Chris Stevens, pilot of the Spitfire on today's sortie

Right PA474 is framed by the BBMF hangar as it is rolled back in after the completion of engine checks. The Coningsby Met have forecast a 30 per cent chance of a lightning strike from the menacing weather, so with the bomber's safety a priority, the Lancaster is pushed undercover

Airshow routine

Left After a slow run past the 100,000 spectators at the Mildenhall Air Fete, *City of Lincoln* gets its undercarriage up ready for a sedate turn before commencing another pass along the runway. PA474 currently bears the code PM-M[2], as worn by a Lancaster of Nos 103 and 576 Sqns. This weary veteran set a Bomber Command record by flying 140 operational sorties during the war. It is the BBMF's intention to change markings regularly to honour every wartime Lancaster unit. The aircraft is due for its next major overhaul during the winter of 1993/94, when the rear and port front spars will be replaced, and it is rumoured that it may re-appear painted up as one of Guy Gibson's Lancasters

Below Overhead the Shuttleworth Collection's Old Warden base in Bedfordshire, the Lancaster shows off its empty bomb bay. A typical wartime bomb load would consist of a mix of incendiaries, a couple of 2000 pounders and one 4000 pounder in the Lancaster's uncomplicated single bomb bay. The mighty aircraft was capable of lifting a load equal to its own weight

Above After its landing roll the Lancaster fast taxies to dispersal at Mildenhall's Air Fete. The BBMF groundcrews double up as gunners during displays to give that air of authenticity to the show

Right PA474 delights the airshow crowds with runs at 100 ft; the fatigue meter on board is carefully monitored after each flight to check that the +1.8 G to -0 barrier is never exceeded

Above The unforgettable sight of the BBMF's Lancaster, Spitfire and Hurricane as they arrive in formation. Approaching the display centreline, the Spitfire and Hurricane break off to leave the stage clear for the Lancaster's solo routine, before returning for their own individual displays

Left PA474 approaches Old Warden Aerodrome at its minimum display height of 100 ft, passing over the country lane that borders the Shuttleworth Collection's grass runways

Above The bomber lines up on finals to Cranfield airfield in 1985

Left PA474 was painted up in the early 1980s to represent the Lancaster flown by Wg Cdr Guy Gibson VC whilst leading No 617 Sqn on the 'Dambusters' raid in 1943. The aircraft used on this epic mission were heavily modified to carry the externally mounted 'bouncing bomb', invented by Barnes Wallis. They were known as Lancaster Mk III 'specials', and to allow them to accommodate a single 9250 lb cylindrically spun weapon, the cavernous bomb bay had to be further cut away

Above PA474 takes off from Cranfield in 1986 wearing the codes of a No 101 Sqn Lancaster

Left The Lancaster is an aircraft that looks right from any angle, and as they say 'if it looks right, it is right'. From the bomber's first flight in January 1941, its designer, the legendary Roy Chadwick, and his design team at A V Roe Ltd, were mystified as to why the aircraft's flight trials went so smoothly, and that the type's performance was better than their predicted values. Many prototype aircraft from this period were downright dangerous during evaluation and test flying, and often required a lot of modification work before they were regarded as suitable for the average service aircrew

Above PA474 as we first saw it in 1973. The aircraft wore the codes KM-B, commemorating the aircraft flown by Sqn Ldr John Nettleton on the daring, but ill-fated, low-level daylight raid on the Mann Diesel factory at Augsburg in April 1942. Nettleton's aircraft was the only one of six Lancasters from No 44 Sqn to return from this mission, four falling to Luftwaffe fighters en route to the target. Sqn Ldr Nettleton was awarded the Victoria Cross for his part in the raid

Left The bomber was minus its mid-upper turret when it first joined the BBMF in 1973; it had been faired over soon after the aircraft was built to accommodate an external saddle tank to extend the range of the aircraft for its proposed role in the Anglo/US Tiger Force operation against the Japanese. A world-wide search for a turret, astrodome and functioning bomb doors was launched, and eventualy these missing parts were discovered by a British businessman at an Argentinian gunnery school. With the aid of funds from the Lincolnshire Lancaster Committee, the parts were brought back to England aboard the *County* class destroyer HMS *Hampshire* in 1973

The BBMF's Lancaster framed over classic English countryside at Old Warden in 1973. This small grass aerodrome which is home to the Shuttleworth Collection is probably the best airshow venue for any visitor to the UK. The Collection operate their own Spitfire Mk Vc (AR501) from this field, and they are currently restoring a Sea Hurricane to flying condition at the Imperial War Museum airfield at Duxford

Above As a reward for their ground marshalling duties, these Air Training Corps cadets get the 'best seats in the house' from which to take photographs of PA474 on finals at the College of Aeronautics at Cranfield, in Bedfordshire

Left Banked-in and with bomb doors open, the Lancaster shows off its current markings and camouflage scheme

Bomber stream

City of Lincoln is escorted by Spitfire Mk Vb AB910 en route to the air display at RNAS Yeovilton. To maximise the utilisation of the Flight, our route took us via RAF Upper Heyford's open house as well. This formation was shot from the rear starboard window aperture of the BBMF'S Devon C.2, cruising at 150 kts. During the Lancaster's first display season over 20,000 Lincolnshire residents signed a petition asking the MoD to base the aircraft permanently in their 'bomber county'. They had to wait a while, but their wish came true in 1975 when PA474 was officially adopted by the City of Lincoln, hence the crest which features so prominantly on its nose. A year later the aircraft, together with the rest of BBMF fleet, was moved from RAF Waddington to its current home in Lincolnshire

Above The pugnacious shape of the Lancaster's nose profile bears the mission symbols of 140 operations flown by PM-M² during its spell with Nos 103 and 576 Sqns. The yellow bombs denote night sorties and the white ones day missions. The red on blue ribbon represents the Distinguished Service Order and the white diagonal the Distinguished Flying Medal; the two swastikas denote a pair of enemy aircraft shot down by 'Taffy' the rear-gunner. PA474's Frazer-Nash Mk 5 nose turret was found in the care of an Air Training Corps unit, who gladly swapped it for a dummy Firestreak missile

Left Once airborne, the large greenhouse-like cockpit becomes a hive of activity, four heads being typically visible at any one time. Pilot and co-pilot are busily formating at 150 kts for the photographer, while the navigator and air engineer check their respective maps and dials from a standing position. Although period navigation equipment is fitted in the aircraft for authenticity, it is disconnected for safety reasons – the navigator has to rely on his maps, a stop-watch and the 'Mk 1 eyeball'. Two modern radios – a V/UHF and VHF – are carried in the aircraft, together with a transponder so that the aircraft's progress can be checked on ground radar more easily. The mid-upper gunner in this photograph obviously doesn't feel under threat from the 'enemy', having swapped his 0.303s for a 35 mm camera

Above Banking away the Lancaster looks heavy. For airshow work the aircraft is flown at a maximum take-off weight of 47,000 lbs, a figure that compares rather favourably with its wartime brothers who would regularly set off for Europe at around the 65,000 lb mark. The fuel load carried during demonstration flights varies between 650 and 950 Imperial gallons, which, when consumed at a rate of 200 gallons per hour, gives the Lancaster a useful endurance of three to four hours with reserves

Right The beautiful and unspoilt island of Sark, measuring about three miles by one and a half, is Europe's last feudal country, being governed by the Seigneur whose rights go back to Queen Elizabeth I and the year 1565. PA474 is escorted over Sark's majestic coastline by the Flight's Griffon-powered Spitfire Mk XIX (PM631). This aircraft is the only BBMF Spitfire not to have seen wartime service, having been built in late 1945. It is currently painted up as a Mk XIV from No 11 Sqn, the unit having flown this version of the Spitfire whilst assigned to South East Asia Command in 1945. These head-on shots were taken from the rear loading ramp of a No 32 Sqn Andover E.3A (XS644), based at RAF Northolt on the outskirts of London. I shared the aircraft with the RAF's parachute display team, 'The Falcons', who are based at RAF Brize Norton in Oxfordshire. After nonchalantly playing Bridge on the flight down to Jersey, they made their own spectacular arrival at the air display by landing 'right on the money' on the narrow stretch of beach at St Peter Port

Above This photograph is reminiscent of a scene from World War 2, as the lumbering bomber crosses the enemy coastline at low-level with its fighter escort. During this sortie the aircraft formated at 130 kts so as to allow the Andover photo-ship to remain within its stipulated ramp down speed band

Left Smile please! As the Lancaster slides under the photo-ship even the weather has improved and everybody is enjoying this wonderfully smooth trip. As the song goes, 'Give me one moment in time' and for those pointing cameras this was that moment; an utterly unforgettable sortie

Previous pages The sign of a good formation pilot; Sqn Ldr Andy Tomalin keeps his eyes glued to the photo-ship, looking for hand signals from the photographer as the Andover captain, Paul Carr, carefully chooses his flight path over some of the most beautiful scenery in the British Isles. Aviation photographers always feel very privileged to be involved in this type of air-to-air sortie – the frustration for the photo-ship pilot is to hear the 'oohs' and 'aahs' in his headset from the photographers at the rear of the aircraft. At the de-briefing Paul Carr simply said, 'I take it that you are fairly pleased' – a typical 'Right Stuff' understatement as he looked at our grinning faces

OK, Now for the finale. My wide angle lens is rapidly strapped on as the triumphant trio come in ever closer and the lens is zoomed back to its stops at 24 mm

FM213

It was on 12 June 1944 at 21.44 hrs that Lancaster VR-A KB726 of No 419 'Moose' Sqn lifted off from No 6 Group Bomber Command base at Middleton-St-George, in northern England. The crew consisted of pilot F/O Arthur de Breyne, wireless operator F/Sgt Jim Kelly, rear gunner F/O Pat Brophy, bomb aimer F/Sgt Jack Friday, navigator F/O Bob Bodie, mid upper gunner P/O Andrew Mynarski and flight engineer F/Sgt Roy Vigars (RAF), who was the only non-Canadian crew member. Their thirteenth operation as a crew was to bomb railway marshalling yards at Cambrai, France, from a dangerously low altitude of 2000 ft.

As the allied bomber stream neared its prescribed target area over France shortly after midnight, the rear gunner sighted a German Ju88G-7 nightfighter and alerted the pilot. F/O de Breyne began evasive action by initiating a corkscrew manoeuvre, spiralling the bomber downward from an altitude of 5000 ft. The Ju88 managed to fire upon the bomber, striking it with three cannon shells. A fuel tank erupted, crippling two engines on the port wing and sparking off a hydraulic oil fire in the aft section of the fuselage. The bomber was doomed.

The order to bail out was given by de Breyne as he struggled to maintain straight and level flight. At the rear of the aircraft, Andrew Mynarski was crawling through flaming hydraulic fluid, fire-axe in hand, in an attempt to save the life of his friend, Pat Brophy, who was trapped in the rear turret. His brave actions were hampered by the intense heat and flames. Brophy recognized that the situation was futile and motioned Mynarski away. Mynarski, in great despair, left his helpless friend and bailed out through the rear escape hatch, his clothing and parachute ablaze. With the outbreak of the fire communication had been severed within the aircraft, F/O de Breyne being unaware of the plight of the rear gunners. He could only assume that they had made their escape. With some difficulty, the rest of the crew, followed by de Breyne, bailed out through the front escape hatch.

KB726 plummeted to earth with its lone passenger caged in the rear turret. The bomb-laden Lancaster broke up on impact without discharging its lethal load, and miraculously released Brophy from his captivity alive.

Right Pilots Bob Hill and Cy Dunbar tuck VR-A in nice and tight, filling the author's lens with the Avro bomber. During VR-A's first ceremonial flight on 24 September 1988, the original fire-axe from KB726 was carried on board. Today, No 419 'Moose' Sqn retains the axe at its base at Cold Lake, Alberta

Above As night bombing ops are no longer a part of VR-A's mission, the exhaust port flame shrouds have been removed

Above right Hunting out the target areas. Capt Bob Hill and co-pilot Don Schofield (with the navigational assistance of ex-RCAF Lancaster bomber pilot George Sobering DFC), look for small town cenotaphs. Every Remembrance Day the CWHM fly VR-A as a tribute to those who served with the allied forces

Right CWHM General Manager Jack Evans looks pensively from the vantage point of the mid-upper gunner's location. It was P/O Andrew Charles Mynarski VC who manned the 'MUG' on the original KB726. VR-A was actually equipped with a Frazer-Nash turret, positioned further aft; today, a Martin 250/CE mounting is fitted in its place

Above VR-A poses silhouetted with its undercarriage down and locked. The aircraft's main landing gear is constructed from original Lancaster drag struts and jacks, combined with Lincoln oleo and wheel assemblies and Shackleton tyres. The tail wheel, tyre and oleo are totally original, however. During VR-A's second test flight a major snag occurred with the hydraulic system, necessitating the use of emergency air bottles to deploy the main landing gear. Needless to say, the safety systems performed flawlessly

Right A bank to starboard shows the classic lines of the Lancaster Mk X. The familiar wartime roundels are visible against the green, earth and black camouflage. Note the low-lead exhaust stains on the leading edge of the starboard wing behind the No 3 engine

Four of the crew (Bodie, Kelly, de Breyne and Brophy) managed to evade enemy captivity with the help of the French underground. Two members (Friday and Vigars) were imprisoned as POWs. Mynarski's burns were so severe that he quickly succumbed to his injuries whilst in the care of French civilians.

Brophy returned to England in September 1944. It was during debriefing that his story was revealed. Because Brophy was the sole witness, further investigation by the Air Ministry was carried out. It was not until October of 1946 that the last Victoria Cross of World War 2 was awarded

Above Hurricane Mk llB YO-A, piloted by Rick Franks (who is the director of the CWHM's flying ops), formates in the shadow of VR-A. This version of the Hurricane was built under licence in Canada by the Canadian Car and Foundry Company. YO-A wears the colours of No 1(F) Sqn (later renumbered as No 401 Sqn), this unit being the first Canadian fighter squadron to serve overseas

Right All of VR-A's engines are matched Packard Merlin 224s, the CWHM acquiring a total of 22 powerplants during the restoration. Sent to the late J R Sandberg's JRS Enterprises machine shop in Minneapolis, Minnesota, all the engines were thoroughly stripped and overhauled. Al Topham, one of the three flight crew chiefs (flight engineers) with the museum, explained that only 75 per cent of maximum power is currently used by the bomber during its routine flying. Circumstances were very different during the war however, Lancasters being regularly subjected to extreme flying conditions, heavy weapons loads and determined nightfighters, factors which were further augmented by adverse attitudes and power settings

Above A rare sight indeed! This photograph was taken in June 1990 from the nose perspex of Dennis Bradley's A-26 Invader. VR-A is leading the pack, with the CWHM's Hurricane, piloted by R J Franks, in line astern to port. Opposing the Hurricane is the Confederate Air Force's Spitfire Mk IX, being capably flown on this occasion by the legendary Howard Pardue, whilst filling the trail slot is Kermit Weeks in his Mosquito B35

Left The glorious sight of eight Merlins purring smoothly at altitude. En route to Centralia (an ex-BCATP airfield), the Lancaster, Mosquito, Spitfire and Hurricane cruise over the farmland of southwestern Ontario

posthumously to P/O Andrew Charles Mynarski for his courage and supreme sacrifice.

The courageous act of the young air gunner was not to be forgotten in the hearts of many Canadians. In June 1984, the Canadian Warplane Heritage Museum at Mount Hope, Ontario, dedicated FM213 (a Lancaster Mk X then being restored by the organization) in memory of P/O Andrew Charles Mynarski VC. The Mynarski Lancaster would become a flying memorial and flagship of the fleet for the museum. Attending the dedication ceremony were crew members from the original VR-A/KB726, and many other RCAF veterans.

Lancaster Mk X KB726/FM213

KB726 was one of 430 Lancaster Mk X airframes to be produced by Victory Aircraft in Malton, Ontario. The initial batch of 300 Lancaster Mk X aircraft built in Canada between August 1943 and March 1945 were assigned manufacturer's numbers between KB700 and KB999. An additional 300 Mk Xs began to roll of the Victory line in April 1945, and these displayed serial numbers beginning at FM100. Shortly after VE Day production of Canadian-built Lancaster Mk Xs was terminated, the last Lancaster to leave the factory wearing the serial FM229. The war took its toll on the Victory Lancasters, no less than 105 aircraft being lost through enemy action between August 1943 and May 1945.

With the cessation of hostilities, the Lancaster was re-tasked within the Royal Canadian Air Force (RCAF). Amongst the post-war bomber fleet was FM213, which had been built in July 1945. This aircraft was equipped with the latest paddle-blade propellers, driven by Packard Merlin 224 two-speed, single-staged, supercharged engines, producing a maximum of 1640 hp each. Like many other factory-fresh Lancasters, FM213 was placed in storage soon after leaving the Victory plant, and left dormant for almost a year.

Nine different Lancaster variants were pressed into service within the post-war RCAF, the ex-Victory bombers being modified by Avro Canada (who had bought out the company soon after the war). These aircraft were designated as Mk 10s, followed by letters indicating their sprcific role. FM213, for example, was converted to Mk 10 MR/MP standards (Maritime Reconnaissance/Maritime Patrol).

Modifications to the airframe included the addition of a 400 gal fuel tank in the bomb bay, deicing boots on the wings, new radar and sonar equipment and the installation of dual controls with improved instrumentation. The typical night bomber camouflage of dark green, earth and black was replaced by an overall silver finish, which was emblazoned with a red fuselage flash and day-glo wing tips and tailplane.

After the completion of all the modifications on FM213 in December 1951, the aircraft was sent to No 405 Sqn in Greenwood, Nova Scotia. While en route to its new squadron, the Lancaster experienced a very heavy landing at Canadian Forces Base (CFB) Trenton, which resulted in FM213 sustaining irreparable damage to its centre section and the main landing gear. The aircraft was disassembled and transported to de Havilland

Right The view from the bomb aimer's position as the Lancaster performs a 'low and over' at Mount Hope

Aircraft at CFB Downsview, where it remained until parts could be found for a rebuild.

KB895, another Lancaster Mk X, was located in the province of Alberta; this aircraft was privately owned by a farmer who had procured the bomber from surplus war stocks. KB895 had served with No 434 'Bluenose' Sqn, stationed at Croft, near York, and following VE Day had returned to Canada along with many other Victory-built Bomber Command veterans. An offer was made to the civilian owner for KB895, which he graciously accepted – the parts salvaged from KB895 would now give FM213 a new lease on life. It was not until August 1953 that FM213 finally arrived at No 405 Sqn at Greenwood, before finally moving on to No 107 Rescue Unit at Torbay, in Newfoundland.

The aircraft led a varied career travelling hundreds of thousands of miles to destinations such as Scotland, Iceland, Bermuda and the Azores. Crews of FM213 performed many tasks including responding to SOS calls from fishing vessels in distress, and answering 'PAN' calls from downed aircraft. On three occasions it flew as an escort for members of the royal family. In October 1963 FM213 was finally retired from active duty with the RCAF. The era of the venerable Lancaster had come to a close, the bomber being replaced by the P2V Neptune and the Argus.

The acquisition of FM213

Goderich, Ontario, was to be FM213's resting place for many years following its retirement from service, thanks to the efforts made by the local branch of the Royal Canadian Legion. They had expressed their concerns about the way the Canadian Forces had been disposing of their remaining Lancaster Mk 10s, most of which had been sold for scrap – a generation of Canadian housewives used aluminium pots and pans that had been manufactured from recycled Lancasters.

Equipped with a valid reason for preservation, coupled with vociferous lobbying, one could convince the government that a Lancaster memorial would be a fitting tribute to those men and women who served their country in war and peace. The members of No 109 Branch of the Royal Canadian Legion certainly proved just that, and without their foresight the weary warrior would never have survived. Upon landing, FM213 was received by Air-Vice Marshall A J Sully, a guard of honour and full colour party. The aircraft spent the next two years of its life in a hangar, waiting for sufficient funds to be raised to enable it to be permanently displayed on pylons. On 15 September 1968, a ceremony took place for FM213, commemorating the British Commonwealth Air Training Plan (BCATP).

Right Lancaster pilot Capt Bob Hill gives a cheerful over-the-shoulder 'mug' for the camera. Having flown a multitude of types including the Chipmunk, Harvard, Expeditor, T-33, CF-100 and CF-101 Voodoo whilst in the RCAF, Bob now commands a Boeing 767 for Air Canada during the week. Prior to checking out in the sophisticated Boeing twin, he flew the DC-4, DC-8, DC-9 and the L-1011. Although flying the Lancaster can hardly be rivalled, he still enjoys open-air flights in the CWHM's PT-17 Stearman

Below right Maintaining a watchful eye on VR-A's flight systems, engineer Gil Hunt is one of three crew chiefs who share the responsibility of monitoring the Lancaster's mechanicals once the Merlins fire up. If you ask the crew chief (or flight engineer, as they were more commonly known during the war) what his list of duties cover, you had better have some time on your hands! Some of the lengthy preflight inspections include checking the control surfaces, and monitoring the fuel, coolant and oil quantity levels. In flight, the crew chief keeps an eye on various engine parameters including temperatures, pressures, pneumatics, fuel flow, voltage and hydraulics, to name but a few!

Unfortunately, the effects of mother nature, coupled with vandalism, began to take its toll on FM213. The legion was suffering from financial troubles as well, and a lack of funds hindered its upkeep. Meanwhile, a few keen individuals had convinced Dennis Bradley that a Lancaster restoration project would be a monumental project for the CWHM to attempt – the foundation had now been laid for the acquisition of Lancaster FM213 from the No 109 Branch of the Royal Canadian Legion.

In July 1977 FM213 was officially handed over to Dennis Bradley. However, the task still remained of moving this large aircraft to the museum at Mount Hope. It seemed that the people who had installed the aircraft on the pylons had been blessed with intuitive foresight however, the three pylons that had been attached to the aircraft – two at the main spar and one at the rear oleo – minimizing the damage inflicted on the airframe whilst it was displayed outdoors. Once off its mounts, an inspection revealed that all four engines were seized, thus removing the option of a ferry flight.

After exhausting all other avenues, the Canadian Armed Forces were called upon to see if they could transport the Lancaster by air to Mount Hope. The airframe had to be stripped down to meet proper weight limitations for an aerial lift before a No 450 Sqn CH-147 Chinook could carry the fuselage and tail section as an underslung load. After two attempts, a successful 1 hour and 40 minute flight was endured. Almost a decade would pass before the aircraft graced the skies once again.

The Canadian Warplane Heritage Museum

The Canadian Warplane Heritage Foundation was established in early 1970 by its current president, Dennis Bradley, and the late Alan Ness – a Fairey Firefly would become the group's first acquisition, and flagship. Interest from local aviation enthusiasts invoked the need for an organized membership. Enthusiastic members, both young and old and from all walks of life, brought their skills, knowledge and talent to the newly formed association.

This non-profit and charitable organization developed into the Canadian Warplane Heritage Museum (CWHM), which is now appropriately housed in the historical hangars of the former BCATP camp at Mount Hope, Ontario.

Now, 20 years on, the CWHM's collection has grown to over 25 aircraft,

Right Juxtaposed against a background that could double for the English Channel, VR-A formates with the Hurricane

Above The view aft from the navigator's astrodome clearly shows the mid-upper gunner's position some distance back

Left A view looking forward from the same vantage point. It is interesting to note that the front half of VR-A's canopy is constructed from one inch diameter stainless steel tubing, and the aft portion is made of spruce wood. This combination prevented the cockpit transparency from interferring with the aircraft's onboard navigational aids

and its membership increased to in excess of 1000 in addition, support clubs have been established for specific aircraft. For example, the Mynarski Memorial Lancaster boasts a support club membership of over 4000 worldwide. The museum has one of the largest collections of airworthy vintage aircraft in the world, all of which are finely restored and flown by dedicated volunteers. Other features include a resource centre housing rare artifacts and publications, and a comprehensive art gallery/gift shop. The base also provides a unique venue for special events and other fundraisers that support the organization.

Every year Mount Hope Airport plays host to the Hamilton International Airshow. The two-day event draws the latest in airborne military hardware from around the world, with the CWHM themselves performing a major part of the historical warbird display and fly past demonstrations. Many affiliated members from across Canada and the USA fly their magnificently restored warbirds to the event to participate in the aerial displays.

On tour

Left Like drones around the 'queen bee', airshow spectators get a splendid opportunity to view VR-A from close quarters as the crew fire up the bomber's engines

Below Harry Huffman keeps a watchful eye on the No 4 engine as the Merlin coughs to life – the men on the ramp remain in contact with VR-A's crew throughout the start-up procedure. At its home base, the Lancaster crew use a typical three-pin collector GPU when firing up the engines to try and conserve the aircraft's battery life as much as possible. On the show circuit VR-A is capable of self start-ups

Above Lancaster VR-A comes to life. Operating temperatures of the engine oil and coolant vary between 50 and 70 degrees C, and 80 to 100 degrees C, respectively. Safe oil capacity per engine, using Mineral 100, is 25 to 35 gallons, whilst normal oil pressure during flight is 60 to 80 lbs

Left Dwarfed by the massive bomber, Harry Huffman monitors the Merlins as they slowly tick over. VR-A's start-up sequence is 4, 3, 2 and 1. Both the outer engines are fitted with generators, whilst numbers 3 and 2 maintain the hydraulics at levels that vary between 200 and 850 lbs psig

Above With the crowd safely marshalled back onto the grass, VR-A's throttles are moved forward for taxying. Four Merlin engines effectively deafen out all other sounds, making conversation futile

Right: Head-on view showing the Lancaster's authentic black underside; wartime Bomber Command aircraft were finished in a matt shade rather than gloss. In preparation for the final painting of VR-A at the end of the aircraft's restoration, a total of four week's worth of 'elbow grease' and 90 gallons of stripper was required. Over a mile of masking tape was applied in six days, along with approximately 78 gallons of paint, which covered all 5600 square feet of the aircraft's surface – the painting of VR-A added a further 500 lbs to the bombers empty weight

Above A total airframe time of 4392 hours was logged on FM213 during its career with the RCAF. Since the bomber's first flight after restoration on 11 September 1988, an additional 322 hours have been chalked up

Left No stranger to the right seat of FM213, Capt Cy Dunbar is one of only five pilots type-rated on the Lancaster in North America

Above left Backtracking after a smooth landing on the grass at Geneseo, New York. Home to one of the largest annual warbird gatherings staged in North America, the modest Geneseo airfiefd regularly welcomes the CWHM Lancaster on its forays 'south of the border'

Left On the take-off roll. The CWHM has prescribed the following guidelines according to which VR-A must be flown: a minimum runway length of 4500 ft, a maximum crosswind component of 15 kts, zero tailwind and a maximum stress of 1.8 G

Above The massive 33 ft bomb doors have been opened on this low pass. FM213 was designed for a bomb load capacity of 12 1000 lb bombs, plus a 4000 lbs 'cookie'; many Lancasters were, however, modified to carry special bomb loads during the war. The maximum speed permissible with the bomb bay doors open is 150 kts, which minimizes the possibility of the skin 'oil-canning'

Above In the pattern VR-A uses 2000 rpm, +1 lb boost, with speeds of 140 kts on the downwind circuit, 125 kts on the base leg and 115 kts on finals, which is eventually slowed to 90 kts as the bomber crosses the threshold. Safety speed limitations with three engines operable, gear down and 15 degrees of flap is 120 kts with 3000 rpm, +7 lbs boost. Operating maximums on climb and dive are 200 kts clean, and 175 kts with gear and flaps extended

Left On the airshow circuit, VR-A touches down in Kamloops, British Columbia – this exotic location happens to be the birth place of the legendary Wg Cdr John 'Moose' Fulton DSO, DFC, AFC. The first RCAF officer to lead a Bomber Command unit into action, Fulton was killed on a raid over Hamburg on 28/29 July 1942 whilst flying a Wellington from No 99 Sqn. A total of 256 bombers were despatched on the raid, 161 of which were Wellingtons – 16 aircraft failed to return. In early 1944 mid-upper gunner F/O Andrew Mynarski VC was posted to No 419 'Moose' Sqn, this famous unit having adopted the late Wg Cdr Fulton's nickname as their own as a mark of respect to their fallen comrade. The third RCAF bomber unit to form overseas during the war, No 419 Sqn's motto in Cree Indian was 'Mossa Aswayita', which loosely translated to read 'Beware of the moose'

Above The grass strip at Geneseo's aerodrome is much kinder to the Lancaster's rubber than the more typical tarmac runways that the bomber encounters in its travels. The aircraft's empty weight, including oil and coolant, is 36,125 lbs; VR-A normally weighs in at between 42,000 to 45,000 lbs, depending on its fuel load. The Lancaster's maximum take-off weight of 53,000 lbs is occasionally reached prior to setting off on long distances trips

Right VR-A heads for the hangar at Mount Hope Airport. In order to preserve the countless hours of restoration, the 'Queen of the fleet' is always hangared

In detail

Left Don't ask a crew chief how many rivets hold the Lancaster together because he will probably tell you to refer to the manual! During peak production at Victory Aircraft the factory built a Lancaster a day, and as with similar assembly lines in the UK, most of the work was done by women

Below The rear-gunner's hydraulically controlled Frazer-Nash turret had four 0.303 in machine guns that were fed ammmunition along disintegrating metal belts

Above A view of the bomb aimer's nose perspex crowned with a pair of 0.303s

Left Rear-gunner F/O Pat Brophy's position in VR-A. Cold and isolated from the other six crew members, the rear-gunner performed a crucial role. Usually the first to spot an enemy attack from the rear, he would advise the pilot on when to take evasive action. The corkscrew manoeuvre was the favoured technique within Bomber Command, the pilot throwing the aircraft into a steep dive in an effort to try and evade the nightfighter; this method was also used when coned by searchlights. As the bomber rapidly lost altitude whilst trying to shake its foe, the pilot had to fight with the controls to regain the aircraft's intended course. The rear-gunner, pinned by the centrifugal force, would usually receive an unforgettable ride!

Above A view of the Mk XIV bomb sight. A continuously set vector was employed from 1943 onwards, and by the use of a mechanical computer, sight and drift were automatically corrected. Unlike previous equipment, the Mk XIV was stabilized, thus allowing the pilot to change the Lancaster's attitude without upsetting the bomb aimer's calculations

Left Looking aft towards the rear-gunner's entry way. Wearing an electrically heated flight suit and gloves, leather flying helmet with head-set and a 'Mae West' type flotation vest, the rear-gunner barely had enough room to breathe, let alone perform his tasks. Because of the lack of space in the turret, the parachute was usually stowed between fuselage formers 40 and 41 on the starboard side. On take-off some gunners would rotate their turrets abeam in case an emergency evacuation was necessary. Complaints of perspex fogging prompted some lads to remove these panels altogether

Above A little 'elbow grease' from Larry Melling keeps VR-A looking pristine. During the war, Flt Lt Melling DFC flew with No 635 Sqn (who were part of No 8 Group's Pathfinder force) from Downham Market, in Norfolk. With seven ops in Halifaxes, and 54 in Lancaster Mk IIIs, Larry is very modest about his wartime service, describing it as 'just something you did'

Right A view down the massive bomb bay. The doors are hydraulically operated, and if the engine-driven pumps or hydraulic system should fail, the pilot simply selects the 'down' position on the bomb bay selector handle and the doors will fall open from their own weight. Drastically low temperatures were encountered during high altitude operations, making onboard systems sluggish and prone to freezing up. To solve this problem engineers incorporated a heating system for the 4000 lb bomb rack, thus preventing the bomb from being 'hung-up'

Above This detail shot highlights the engine magneto toggle switches

Left A view of the throttle and propeller speed control assembly. When the engines are fully opened up VR-A develops an overwhelming 6480 hp from its four supercharged Packard Merlin 224s

Previous pages Although wartime Lancasters were only equipped with single flying controls, modifications after the war saw many cockpits converted over to dual systems. VR-A is flown by two type-rated pilots at all times

Above left The front portion of the canopy does not have wipers, the transparency being kept clear and frost free by a pair of deicing spray nozzles fed from a glycol reservoir

Above right This view of the port vertical fin clearly shows its immense size. The combined control surface area of the bomber's fins and rudders is 111.4 sq ft

The crew is always watched by the 'Moose', the official mascot of No 419 Sqn. You will never hear a complaint from this honourable little crew member!

Above Check that tyre pressure! LAC Norman 'Kit' Carson's career has come full circle – as a groundcrewman during the war, Kit was initially stationed at Leeming, near Croft, and finally at Middleton-St-George with No 419 Sqn. An expert on the classic Avro bomber, Kit believes that the only real difference between VR-A and the wartime Lancasters that he serviced concern the fitment of FM213's engine cowlings. 'They went on real nice. They were new Lancs!' As there are only two flying Lancasters left in the world, the CWHM maintains close contacts with the BBMF as anomalies occasionally arise and notes need to be compared. For example, recent conversations with the Flight have lead to the main undercarriage tyre pressures being increased from 45 PSI to 60 PSI in an effort to further reduce the stress placed on the fuselage during landing

Left The Lancaster is equipped with split trailing edge landing flaps capable of a maximum deflection of 56.5 degrees. Hydraulically operated, the flaps can either be fully extended or stepped. The pilot may select any desired angle, this being achieved by returning the flap selector lever to the neutral position

Veterans

Left Capt Bob Hill keeps a watchful eye on the exhaust from the No 2 Merlin. The first pilots to fly VR-A/FM213 following its restoration were Sqn Ldr Tony Banfield of the BBMF, and Capt Hill

Below 'Lets get it straight. Port is left and starboard's right, eh?!' In September 1988, following a 26-year break, Capt Stew Brickenden (right) once again finds himself at the controls of a Lancaster. An ex-RCAF squadron leader, he has accumulated in excess of 20,000 flying hours; Brickenden's log book includes time on the Albatross, Dakota, CF-100 (which happens to be his favourite because 'jets are easy to fly') and the B-25. Today he flies executive jets on a management contract basis. At the museum it is not unusual to see him flying two different aircraft on the same day. Flying alongside him on this sortie is Capt Hill

Left The telltale white flying scarf of rear-gunner Fred Passmore lists all 34 combat missions that he participated in with No 428 Sqn out of Middleton-St-George

Below Throughout the year many interviews are conducted at the museum; here F/O Passmore gets to tell his story

Right F/O Passmore brushes the dust off the old kit and demonstrates the bulkiness of the rear-gunner's attire. He recalls the frenzy of one mission during which a round of 'friendly fire' grazed his head. As Fred put it, 'I was damned lucky I didn't get killed'

Below Back in the saddle again. Capt Cy Dunbar first flew FM213 whilst on active duty for the RCAF in 1957 – he has to his credit a total of 2600 hours PIC on Lancasters, 600 of them on FM213. Throughout his flying career Cy has logged hours in various aircraft in addition to the Lancaster, including such types as the Harvard, Vampire, Expeditor, DC-3, Neptune, Argus, Herald, HS 748 and the Boeing 737. Currently chief CWHM Lancaster pilot, Capt Dunbar now occupies the same seat that he did over 30 years ago

Left Clutching a prop dome puller, Steve Martin AME is one of two full-time engineers employed by the museum. Most of VR-A's maintenance is performed by volunteers, some of whom are retired from active duty

Below Gil Hunt gives the thumbs-up, indicating that VR-A is ready for the off. The enormous canopy on the Lancaster contributes to a phenomenon known as the 'green house effect', which, on a hot summer's day, can leave the crew feeling decidedly parched even before the bomber has left the runway

Below The 'Geritol' crew takes a break. While on the airshow circuit a few years back, it was noted that members of the VR-A crew were on average about 68 years of age, a fact which soon earnt them their nickname. However, contrary to popular belief, this team has more energy packed into it than any amount of Geritol. As a member of the RCAF, LAC Harry Huffman (left) served two months with Nos 76 and 78 Sqns at Linton-on-Ouse. When No 434 Sqn was forming up, Harry became one of its first members. Knowledgeable on Hercules and Merlin engines, LAC Huffman is a valuable asset to VR-A. Al Topham (right) is one of the Lancaster's crew chiefs. Hailing from Liverpool in England, Al's interest in aviation originates from childhood when he was an air cadet. In 1942/43 he was in the Home Guard as an anti-aircraft gunner, following which he was posted to the 8th Army Intelligence Section in Italy. Now retired, Al is fulfilling his life-long passion through his association with the CWHM

Left Gil in the saddle of the trusty mule. The delicate task of moving 20 tons of Lancaster back into its hangar requires all the skill and patience of the crew. Gil Hunt saw service with No 116 Sqn, Coastal Command, as a flight engineer on the PBY-5A Canso. Performing anti-shipping and convoy coverage, he travelled to places such as the Bahamas, Bermuda, the Azores, Iceland and Wick in Scotland

Below Hot, tasty, and plenty of it! On weekends the Lancaster Support Club is always ready to serve up a variety of culinary delights in the Krakow Wing

Right While Gord Hill tunes in for the latest reports from Bomber Command on the R-1155, Museum Research Curator Rob Schweyer performs some investigative work in the background. The Museum houses an extensive research library full of rare aviation memorabilia

Below A proud crew and its precious metal. It is the interest, strength and determination of the regular members and various support groups that keep the dreams alive at the Canadian Warplane Heritage Museum

A salute to three decorated veterans of Bomber Command. From left to right, F/O Bill Randall CD, RCAF, who served as a Lancaster pilot with Nos 576 and 150 Sqns, flying a total of 31 ops. Bill's most vivid memories are the night flights; 'While the sun was setting behind the bomber stream as we headed into the night sky, distant flashes could be seen on the ground as the V2 rockets lifted off into the twilight sky, leaving behind long white jagged vapour trails as they travelled through various moving air masses. I thought it was as eerie as hell!' Today, Bill is the chair of the Lancaster Support Club, and as such he can often be seen carrying around his portable office – a briefcase filled with Lancaster facts and support club information. Flt Lt Larry Melling DFC served in the RAF with No 4 Group, flying seven missions in Halifax Mk IIIs, before being posted to Downham Market with No 8 Group Pathfinders. Whilst based in Norfolk he flew a further 54 sorties in Lancaster Mk IIIs. Larry and Bill made an unusual discovery in 1988 whilst comparing their logbooks; during a daylight raid in March 1945, they shared the same operational target over Bremen, their Lancasters being separated by 33 seconds on the bomb run. Like many other wartime Canadian pilots, George Sobering DFC was attached to the RAF, flying 35 missions in Lancasters with No 115 Sqn at Ely, near Cambridge. Although he is both a director on the museum's board and secretary treasurer of the Lancaster Support Club, he still finds time to head the Spitfire acquisition committee as well

Above The main entrance to the CWH Museum at Mount Hope, Ontario

Above left Can this be real? Hailing from Dayton, Ohio, these members of the Association of Living History, wearing authentic RAF Bomber Command period garb, pose for a 'snap' alongside VR-A. Each member is well versed in the role represented by his or her respective uniform and wing

Left Commonly referred to around Mount Hope as the 'Beech Boys', pilots Paul Cronkwright (left) and Bob McKinnon (right) pose in front of the CWHM's Beechcraft Expeditor. The venerable 'bug-smasher' served as a luxurious photographic platform for many of the air-to-air shots which feature in this volume. This Expeditor is a model D18-S, built in 1946 and powered by 'Mr Pratt & Mrs Whitney', as Bob refers to them. These P & W Junior 985s are rated at 450 hp each, giving the aircraft a maximum speed of 225 mph

Technical Specification

Avro Lancaster B Mk III Cutaway Drawing Key

1 Two 0.303-in (7,7-mm) Browning machine-guns
2 Frazer-Nash power-operated nose turret
3 Nose blister
4 Bomb-aimer's panel (optically flat)
5 Bomb-aimer's control panel
6 Side windows
7 External air temperature thermometer
8 Pitot head
9 Bomb-aimer's chest support
10 Fire extinguisher
11 Parachute emergency exit
12 F.24 camera
13 Glycol tank/step
14 Ventilator fairing
15 Bomb-bay doors forward actuating jacks
16 Bomb-bay forward bulkhead
17 Control linkage
18 Rudder pedals
19 Instrument panel
20 Windscreen sprays
21 Windscreen
22 Dimmer switches
23 Flight-engineer's folding seat
24 Flight engineer's control panel
25 Pilot's seat
26 Flight-deck floor level
27 Elevator and rudder control rods (underfloor)
28 Trim tab control cables
29 Main floor/bomb-bay support longeron
30 Fire extinguisher
31 Wireless installation
32 Navigator's seat
33 Canopy rear/down-view blister
34 Pilot's head armour
35 Cockpit canopy emergency escape hatch
36 D/F loop
37 Aerial mast support
38 Electrical services panel
39 Navigator's compartment window
40 Navigator's desk
41 Aircraft and radio compass receiver
42 Wireless-operator's desk
43 Wireless-operator's seat
44 Wireless-operator's compartment window
45 Front spar carry-through/ fuselage frame
46 Astrodome
47 Inboard section wing ribs
48 Spar join
49 Aerial mast
50 Starboard inboard engine nacelle
51 Spinner
52 Three-blade De Havilland constant-speed propellers
53 Oil cooler intake
54 Oil cooler radiator
55 Carburettor air intake
56 Radiator shutter
57 Engine bearer frame
58 Exhaust flame-damper shroud
59 Packard-built Rolls-Royce Merlin 28 liquid-cooled engine
60 Nacelle/wing fairing
61 Fuel tank bearer ribs
62 Intermediate ribs
63 Leading-edge structure
64 Wing stringers
65 Wingtip skinning
66 Starboard navigation light
67 Starboard formation light
68 Aileron hinge fairings
69 Wing rear spar
70 Starboard aileron
71 Aileron balance tab
72 Balance tab control rod
73 Aileron trim tab
74 HF aerial
75 Split trailing-edge flap (outboard section)
76 Emergency (ditching) exit
77 Crash axe stowage
78 Fire extinguisher
79 Hydraulic reservoir
80 Signal/flare pistol stowage
81 Parachute stowage box/spar step
82 Rear spar carry-through
83 Bunk backrest
84 Rear spar fuselage frame
85 Emergency packs
86 Roof light
87 Dinghy manual release cable (dinghy stowage in starboard wing root)
88 Mid-gunner's parachute stowage
89 Tail turret ammunition box
90 Ammunition feed track
91 Emergency (ditching) exit
92 Flame floats stowage
93 Sea markers stowage
94 Roof light
95 Dorsal turret fairing

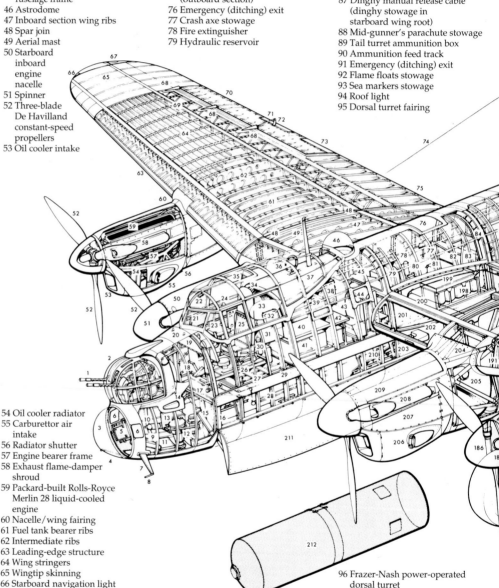

96 Frazer-Nash power-operated dorsal turret
97 Two 0.303-in (7,7-mm) Browning machine guns

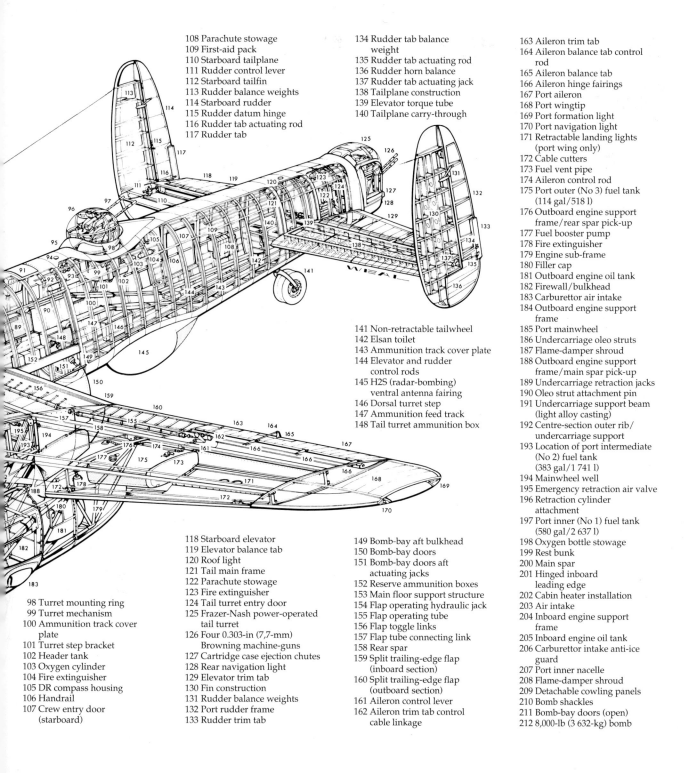

108 Parachute stowage
109 First-aid pack
110 Starboard tailplane
111 Rudder control lever
112 Starboard tailfin
113 Rudder balance weights
114 Starboard rudder
115 Rudder datum hinge
116 Rudder tab actuating rod
117 Rudder tab

134 Rudder tab balance
    weight
135 Rudder tab actuating rod
136 Rudder horn balance
137 Rudder tab actuating jack
138 Tailplane construction
139 Elevator torque tube
140 Tailplane carry-through

163 Aileron trim tab
164 Aileron balance tab control
    rod
165 Aileron balance tab
166 Aileron hinge fairings
167 Port aileron
168 Port wingtip
169 Port formation light
170 Port navigation light
171 Retractable landing lights
    (port wing only)
172 Cable cutters
173 Fuel vent pipe
174 Aileron control rod
175 Port outer (No 3) fuel tank
    (114 gal/518 l)
176 Outboard engine support
    frame/rear spar pick-up
177 Fuel booster pump
178 Fire extinguisher
179 Engine sub-frame
180 Filler cap
181 Outboard engine oil tank
182 Firewall/bulkhead
183 Carburettor air intake
184 Outboard engine support
    frame

141 Non-retractable tailwheel
142 Elsan toilet
143 Ammunition track cover plate
144 Elevator and rudder
    control rods
145 H2S (radar-bombing)
    ventral antenna fairing
146 Dorsal turret step
147 Ammunition feed track
148 Tail turret ammunition box

185 Port mainwheel
186 Undercarriage oleo struts
187 Flame-damper shroud
188 Outboard engine support
    frame/main spar pick-up
189 Undercarriage retraction jacks
190 Oleo strut attachment pin
191 Undercarriage support beam
    (light alloy casting)
192 Centre-section outer rib/
    undercarriage support
193 Location of port intermediate
    (No 2) fuel tank
    (383 gal/1 741 l)
194 Mainwheel well
195 Emergency retraction air valve
196 Retraction cylinder
    attachment
197 Port inner (No 1) fuel tank
    (580 gal/2 637 l)
198 Oxygen bottle stowage
199 Rest bunk
200 Main spar
201 Hinged inboard
    leading edge
202 Cabin heater installation
203 Air intake
204 Inboard engine support
    frame
205 Inboard engine oil tank
206 Carburettor intake anti-ice
    guard
207 Port inner nacelle
208 Flame-damper shroud
209 Detachable cowling panels
210 Bomb shackles
211 Bomb-bay doors (open)
212 8,000-lb (3 632-kg) bomb

98 Turret mounting ring
99 Turret mechanism
100 Ammunition track cover
    plate
101 Turret step bracket
102 Header tank
103 Oxygen cylinder
104 Fire extinguisher
105 DR compass housing
106 Handrail
107 Crew entry door
    (starboard)

118 Starboard elevator
119 Elevator balance tab
120 Roof light
121 Tail main frame
122 Parachute stowage
123 Fire extinguisher
124 Tail turret entry door
125 Frazer-Nash power-operated
    tail turret
126 Four 0.303-in (7,7-mm)
    Browning machine-guns
127 Cartridge case ejection chutes
128 Rear navigation light
129 Elevator trim tab
130 Fin construction
131 Rudder balance weights
132 Port rudder frame
133 Rudder trim tab

149 Bomb-bay aft bulkhead
150 Bomb-bay doors
151 Bomb-bay doors aft
    actuating jacks
152 Reserve ammunition boxes
153 Main floor support structure
154 Flap operating hydraulic jack
155 Flap operating tube
156 Flap toggle links
157 Flap tube connecting link
158 Rear spar
159 Split trailing-edge flap
    (inboard section)
160 Split trailing-edge flap
    (outboard section)
161 Aileron control lever
162 Aileron trim tab control
    cable linkage

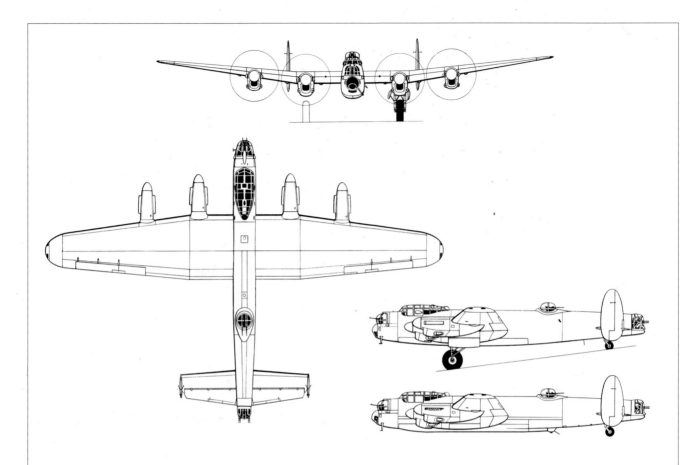

LANCASTER B MK 1

Type: seven-seat heavy bomber

Engines: four 1460 hp Rolls-Royce or Packard Merlin 20 or 22 engines (Mk II only fitted with four Bristol Hercules VI, 14 cylinder two-row, sleeve-valve radials)

Dimensions: span 102 ft (31.1 metres); length 69 ft 4 in (21.1 metres); height 19 ft 7 in (5.97 metres)

Weights: empty 36,900 lbs (16,705 kg); loaded 68,000 (30,800 kg); overloaded with a 22,000 lb bomb 70,000 lbs (31,750 kg)

Performance: maximum speed of 287 mph (462 km/h) at 11,500 ft (3500 metres); cruising speed of 210 mph (338 km/h); climb at maximum weight to 20,000 ft (6095 metres) in 41 minutes; service ceiling 24,500 ft (7467 metres); range with 14,000 lbs (6350 kg) of bombs 1660 miles (2675 km)

Armament: nose and dorsal turret (sometimes also ventral) fitted with two 0.303 in Brownings (some, including the Mk VII, had Martin dorsal turrets with a pair of 0.50 in Brownings fitted instead); tail turret equipped with four 0.303 in Brownings; 33 ft (10.06 metre) bomb bay carrying normal load of 14,000 lbs (6350 kg) or 22,000 lbs (9979 kg) of bombs with special modification

History: first flight 9 January 1941, followed by first service delivery in September of the same year; last delivery from new on 2 February 1946